OTIS DESIGNS

BLOOMS & BUTTERFLIES

2024

COLORING GOAL
PLANNER

ADAPTED FROM PHOTOGRAPHY
BY AMANDA OTIS

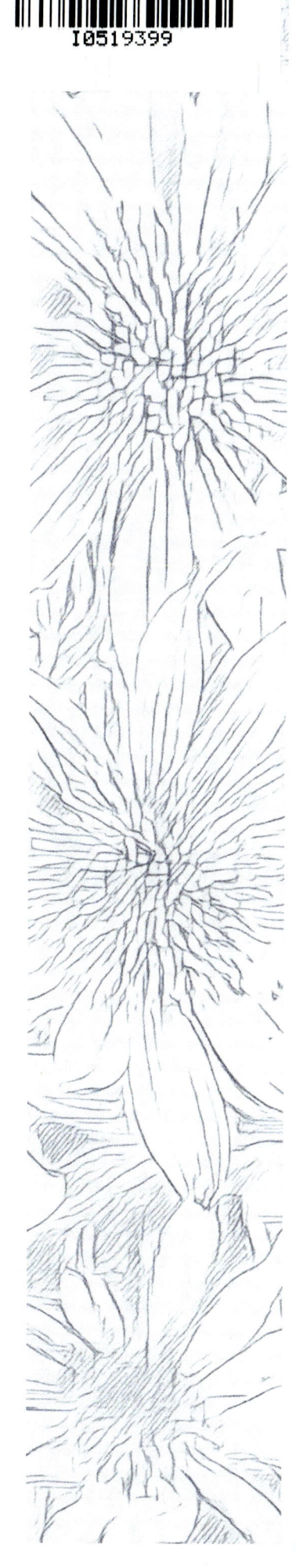

JAN

S	M	T	W	T	F	S
	1	2	3	4	5	6
7	8	9	10	11	12	13
14	15	16	17	18	19	20
21	22	23	24	25	26	27
28	29	30	31			

FEB

S	M	T	W	T	F	S
				1	2	3
4	5	6	7	8	9	10
11	12	13	14	15	16	17
18	19	20	21	22	23	24
25	26	27	28	29		

MAR

S	M	T	W	T	F	S
					1	2
3	4	5	6	7	8	9
10	11	12	13	14	15	16
17	18	19	20	21	22	23
24	25	26	27	28	29	30
31						

APR

S	M	T	W	T	F	S
	1	2	3	4	5	6
7	8	9	10	11	12	13
14	15	16	17	18	19	20
21	22	23	24	25	26	27
28	29	30				

MAY

S	M	T	W	T	F	S
			1	2	3	4
5	6	7	8	9	10	11
12	13	14	15	16	17	18
19	20	21	22	23	24	25
26	27	28	29	30	31	

JUN

S	M	T	W	T	F	S
						1
2	3	4	5	6	7	8
9	10	11	12	13	14	15
16	17	18	19	20	21	22
23	24	25	26	27	28	29
30						

JUL

S	M	T	W	T	F	S
	1	2	3	4	5	6
7	8	9	10	11	12	13
14	15	16	17	18	19	20
21	22	23	24	25	26	27
28	29	30	31			

AUG

S	M	T	W	T	F	S
				1	2	3
4	5	6	7	8	9	10
11	12	13	14	15	16	17
18	19	20	21	22	23	24
25	26	27	28	29	30	31

SEP

S	M	T	W	T	F	S
1	2	3	4	5	6	7
8	9	10	11	12	13	14
15	16	17	18	19	20	21
22	23	24	25	26	27	28
29	30					

OCT

S	M	T	W	T	F	S
		1	2	3	4	5
6	7	8	9	10	11	12
13	14	15	16	17	18	19
20	21	22	23	24	25	26
27	28	29	30	31		

NOV

S	M	T	W	T	F	S
					1	2
3	4	5	6	7	8	9
10	11	12	13	14	15	16
17	18	19	20	21	22	23
24	25	26	27	28	29	30

DEC

S	M	T	W	T	F	S
1	2	3	4	5	6	7
8	9	10	11	12	13	14
15	16	17	18	19	20	21
22	23	24	25	26	27	28
29	30	31				

January 2024

Planner

SUNDAY	MONDAY	TUESDAY	WEDNESDAY	THURSDAY	FRIDAY	SATURDAY
31	01	02	03	04	05	06
07	08	09	10	11	12	13
14	15	16	17	18	19	20
21	22	23	24	25	26	27
28	29	30	31	01	02	03

JANUARY GOALS

GOAL

STRATEGY

_____
_____
_____
_____
_____
_____
_____
_____
_____
_____
_____
_____
_____

ACTION STEPS

1 _____
2 _____
3 _____
4 _____
5 _____

Created   /   /   To Achieve By   /   /   Achieved ○

GOAL

STRATEGY

_____
_____
_____
_____
_____
_____
_____
_____
_____
_____
_____
_____

ACTION STEPS

1 _____
2 _____
3 _____
4 _____
5 _____

Created   /   /   To Achieve By   /   /   Achieved ○

Weekly

Goals for this week

01 _____
02 _____
03 _____
04 _____
05 _____
06 _____
07 _____

To do list

01 _____
02 _____
03 _____
04 _____
05 _____
06 _____
07 _____

Notes

_____
_____
_____
_____
_____
_____
_____
_____
_____
_____
_____

Sunday

Monday

Tuesday

Wednesday

Thursday

Friday

Saturday

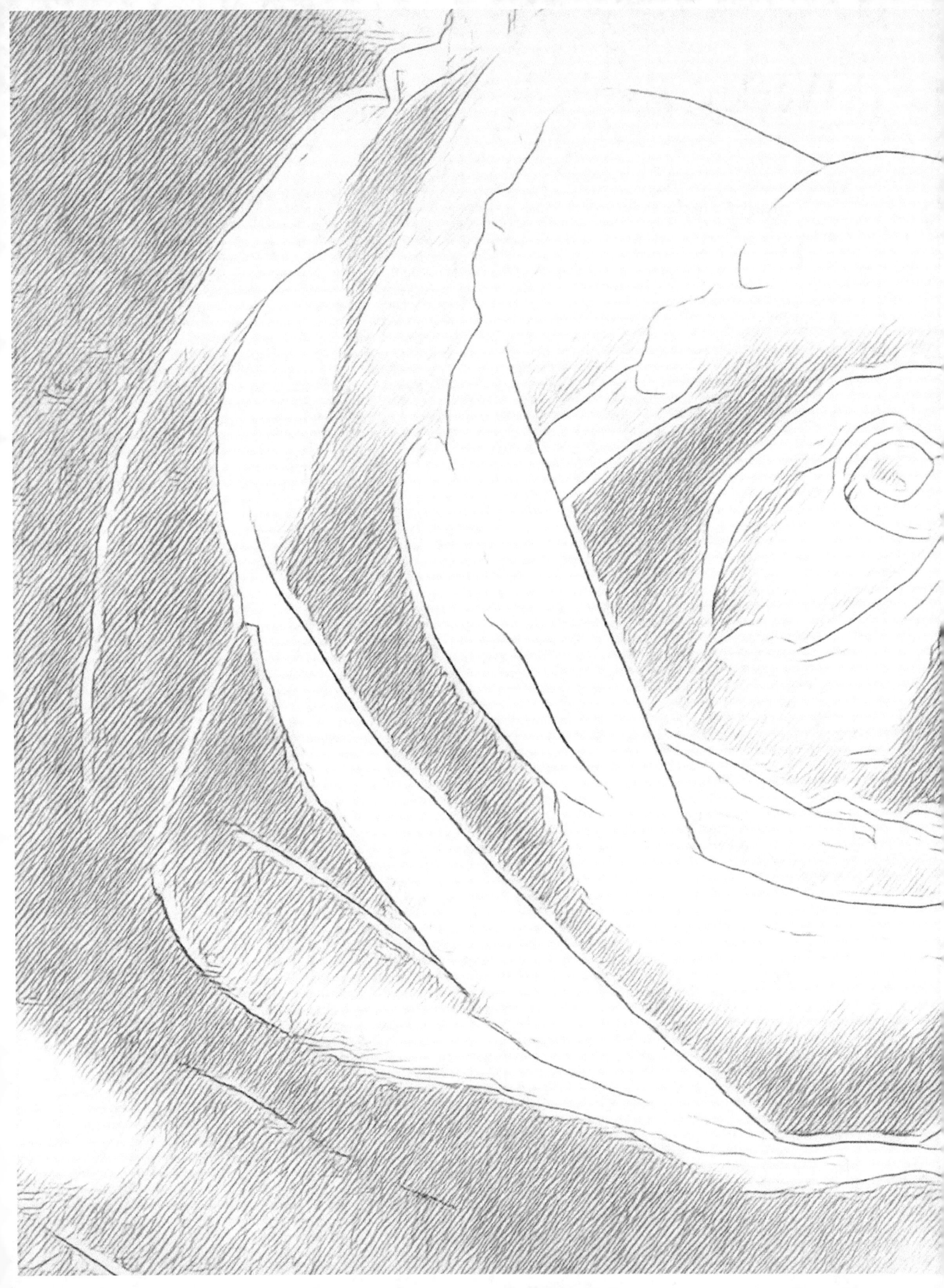

Weekly

Goals for this week

01 _____
02 _____
03 _____
04 _____
05 _____
06 _____
07 _____

To do list

01 _____
02 _____
03 _____
04 _____
05 _____
06 _____
07 _____

Notes

_____
_____
_____
_____
_____
_____
_____
_____
_____
_____
_____
_____

Sunday

Monday

Tuesday

Wednesday

Thursday

Friday

Saturday

Weekly

Goals for this week

01 _____
02 _____
03 _____
04 _____
05 _____
06 _____
07 _____

To do list

01 _____
02 _____
03 _____
04 _____
05 _____
06 _____
07 _____

Notes

_____
_____
_____
_____
_____
_____
_____
_____
_____
_____
_____

Sunday

Monday

Tuesday

Wednesday

Thursday

Friday

Saturday

Weekly

Planner

Goals for this week

01 _____
02 _____
03 _____
04 _____
05 _____
06 _____
07 _____

To do list

01 _____
02 _____
03 _____
04 _____
05 _____
06 _____
07 _____

Notes

_____
_____
_____
_____
_____
_____
_____
_____
_____
_____
_____

Sunday

Monday

Tuesday

Wednesday

Thursday

Friday

Saturday

Weekly

Goals for this week

01 _____
02 _____
03 _____
04 _____
05 _____
06 _____
07 _____

To do list

01 _____
02 _____
03 _____
04 _____
05 _____
06 _____
07 _____

Notes

_____
_____
_____
_____
_____
_____
_____
_____
_____
_____
_____

Sunday

Monday

Tuesday

Wednesday

Thursday

Friday

Saturday

February 2024

Planner

SUNDAY	MONDAY	TUESDAY	WEDNESDAY	THURSDAY	FRIDAY	SATURDAY
28	29	30	31	01	02	03
04	05	06	07	08	09	10
11	12	13	14	15	16	17
18	19	20	21	22	23	24
25	26	27	28	29	01	02

FEBRUARY GOALS

GOAL

STRATEGY

ACTION STEPS

1
2
3
4
5

Created   /   /   To Achieve By   /   /   Achieved ○

GOAL

STRATEGY

ACTION STEPS

1
2
3
4
5

Created   /   /   To Achieve By   /   /   Achieved ○

Weekly

Goals for this week

01 _____
02 _____
03 _____
04 _____
05 _____
06 _____
07 _____

To do list

01 _____
02 _____
03 _____
04 _____
05 _____
06 _____
07 _____

Notes

_____
_____
_____
_____
_____
_____
_____
_____
_____
_____
_____
_____

Sunday

Monday

Tuesday

Wednesday

Thursday

Friday

Saturday

Weekly
 Planner

Goals for this week

01 _____
02 _____
03 _____
04 _____
05 _____
06 _____
07 _____

To do list

01 _____
02 _____
03 _____
04 _____
05 _____
06 _____
07 _____

Notes

_____
_____
_____
_____
_____
_____
_____
_____
_____
_____
_____

Sunday

Monday

Tuesday

Wednesday

Thursday

Friday

Saturday

Weekly

Planner

Goals for this week

01 _____
02 _____
03 _____
04 _____
05 _____
06 _____
07 _____

To do list

01 _____
02 _____
03 _____
04 _____
05 _____
06 _____
07 _____

Notes

_____
_____
_____
_____
_____
_____
_____
_____
_____
_____
_____

Sunday

Monday

Tuesday

Wednesday

Thursday

Friday

Saturday

Weekly

Goals for this week

01
02
03
04
05
06
07

To do list

01
02
03
04
05
06
07

Notes

_____
_____
_____
_____
_____
_____
_____
_____
_____
_____
_____

Sunday

Monday

Tuesday

Wednesday

Thursday

Friday

Saturday

Weekly

Goals for this week

01 _____
02 _____
03 _____
04 _____
05 _____
06 _____
07 _____

To do list

01 _____
02 _____
03 _____
04 _____
05 _____
06 _____
07 _____

Notes

_____
_____
_____
_____
_____
_____
_____
_____
_____
_____
_____

Sunday

Monday

Tuesday

Wednesday

Thursday

Friday

Saturday

March 2024

Planner

SUNDAY	MONDAY	TUESDAY	WEDNESDAY	THURSDAY	FRIDAY	SATURDAY
25	26	27	28	29	01	02
03	04	05	06	07	08	09
10	11	12	13	14	15	16
17	18	19	20	21	22	23
24	25	26	27	28	29	30
31	01	02	03	04	05	06

MARCH GOALS

GOAL

STRATEGY

ACTION STEPS

1
2
3
4
5

Created   /   /   To Achieve By   /   /   Achieved ◯

GOAL

STRATEGY

ACTION STEPS

1
2
3
4
5

Created   /   /   To Achieve By   /   /   Achieved ◯

Weekly

Planner

Goals for this week

01 _____
02 _____
03 _____
04 _____
05 _____
06 _____
07 _____

To do list

01 _____
02 _____
03 _____
04 _____
05 _____
06 _____
07 _____

Notes

_____
_____
_____
_____
_____
_____
_____
_____
_____
_____
_____
_____

Sunday

Monday

Tuesday

Wednesday

Thursday

Friday

Saturday

Weekly

Goals for this week

01 _____
02 _____
03 _____
04 _____
05 _____
06 _____
07 _____

To do list

01 _____
02 _____
03 _____
04 _____
05 _____
06 _____
07 _____

Notes

_____
_____
_____
_____
_____
_____
_____
_____
_____
_____
_____

Sunday

Monday

Tuesday

Wednesday

Thursday

Friday

Saturday

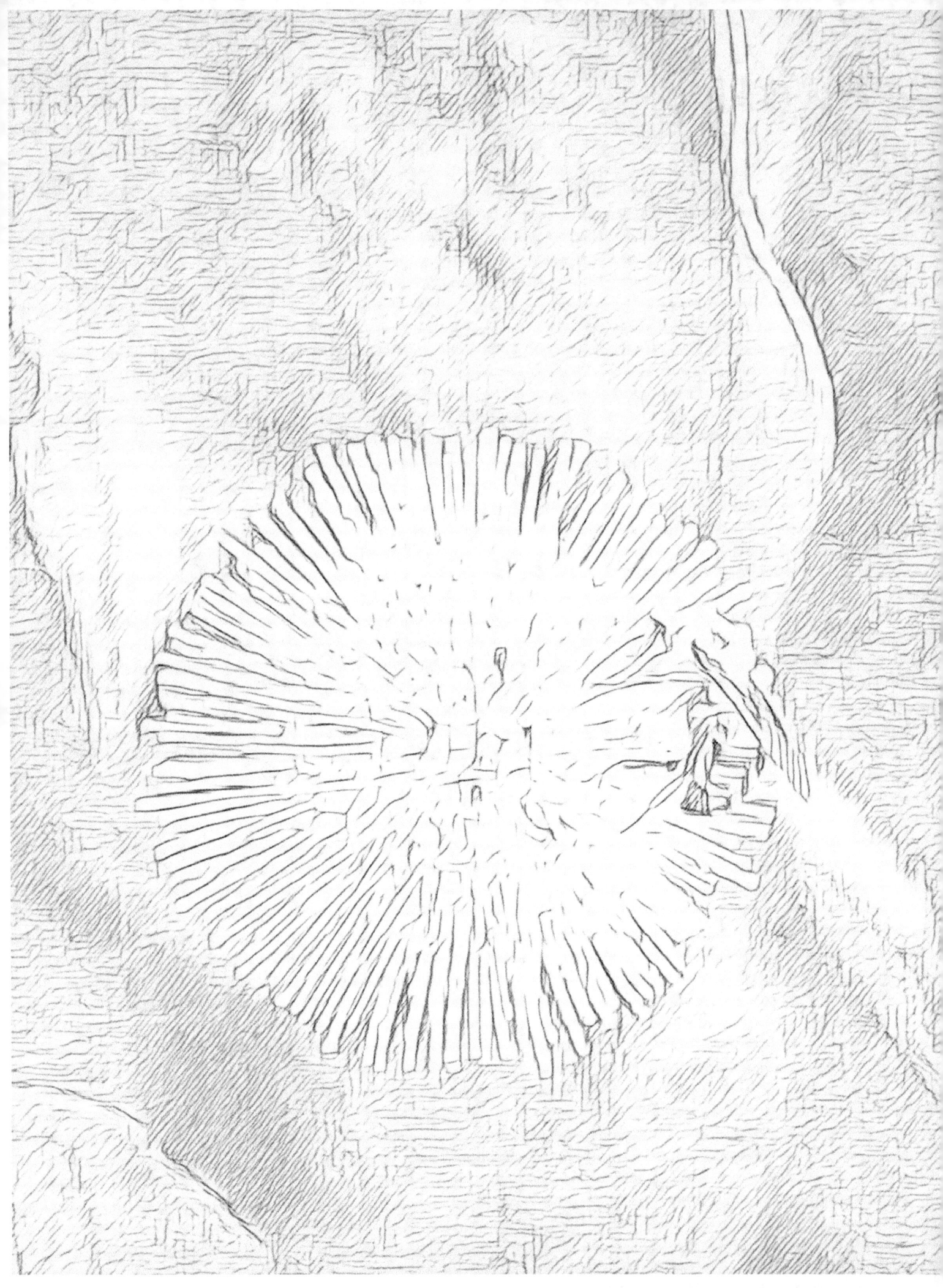

Weekly

Goals for this week

01 _____
02 _____
03 _____
04 _____
05 _____
06 _____
07 _____

To do list

01 _____
02 _____
03 _____
04 _____
05 _____
06 _____
07 _____

Notes

_____
_____
_____
_____
_____
_____
_____
_____
_____
_____
_____
_____

Sunday

Monday

Tuesday

Wednesday

Thursday

Friday

Saturday

Weekly

Goals for this week

01
02
03
04
05
06
07

To do list

01
02
03
04
05
06
07

Notes

Sunday

Monday

Tuesday

Wednesday

Thursday

Friday

Saturday

Weekly

Planner

Goals for this week

01
02
03
04
05
06
07

To do list

01
02
03
04
05
06
07

Notes

Sunday

Monday

Tuesday

Wednesday

Thursday

Friday

Saturday

April 2024

Planner

SUNDAY	MONDAY	TUESDAY	WEDNESDAY	THURSDAY	FRIDAY	SATURDAY
31	01	02	03	04	05	06
07	08	09	10	11	12	13
14	15	16	17	18	19	20
21	22	23	24	25	26	27
28	29	30	01	02	03	04

APRIL GOALS

GOAL

STRATEGY

ACTION STEPS

1
2
3
4
5

Created   /   /   To Achieve By   /   /   Achieved ◯

GOAL

STRATEGY

ACTION STEPS

1
2
3
4
5

Created   /   /   To Achieve By   /   /   Achieved ◯

Weekly

Planner

Goals for this week

01 _____
02 _____
03 _____
04 _____
05 _____
06 _____
07 _____

To do list

01 _____
02 _____
03 _____
04 _____
05 _____
06 _____
07 _____

Notes

_____
_____
_____
_____
_____
_____
_____
_____
_____
_____
_____

Sunday

Monday

Tuesday

Wednesday

Thursday

Friday

Saturday

Weekly

Goals for this week

01 _____
02 _____
03 _____
04 _____
05 _____
06 _____
07 _____

To do list

01 _____
02 _____
03 _____
04 _____
05 _____
06 _____
07 _____

Notes

_____
_____
_____
_____
_____
_____
_____
_____
_____
_____
_____
_____

Sunday

Monday

Tuesday

Wednesday

Thursday

Friday

Saturday

Weekly

Goals for this week

01 _____
02 _____
03 _____
04 _____
05 _____
06 _____
07 _____

To do list

01 _____
02 _____
03 _____
04 _____
05 _____
06 _____
07 _____

Notes

_____
_____
_____
_____
_____
_____
_____
_____
_____
_____
_____
_____

Sunday

Monday

Tuesday

Wednesday

Thursday

Friday

Saturday

Weekly

Goals for this week

01 _____
02 _____
03 _____
04 _____
05 _____
06 _____
07 _____

To do list

01 _____
02 _____
03 _____
04 _____
05 _____
06 _____
07 _____

Notes

_____
_____
_____
_____
_____
_____
_____
_____
_____
_____
_____
_____

Sunday

Monday

Tuesday

Wednesday

Thursday

Friday

Saturday

Weekly
 *Planner*

Goals for this week

01 _____
02 _____
03 _____
04 _____
05 _____
06 _____
07 _____

To do list

01 _____
02 _____
03 _____
04 _____
05 _____
06 _____
07 _____

Notes

_____
_____
_____
_____
_____
_____
_____
_____
_____
_____
_____
_____
_____

Sunday

Monday

Tuesday

Wednesday

Thursday

Friday

Saturday

May 2024

Planner

SUNDAY	MONDAY	TUESDAY	WEDNESDAY	THURSDAY	FRIDAY	SATURDAY
28	29	30	01	02	03	04
05	06	07	08	09	10	11
12	13	14	15	16	17	18
19	20	21	22	23	24	25
26	27	28	29	30	31	01

MAY GOALS

GOAL

ACTION STEPS

1
2
3
4
5

STRATEGY

Created   /   /   To Achieve By   /   /   Achieved ◯

GOAL

ACTION STEPS

1
2
3
4
5

STRATEGY

Created   /   /   To Achieve By   /   /   Achieved ◯

Weekly

Planner

Goals for this week

01 _____
02 _____
03 _____
04 _____
05 _____
06 _____
07 _____

To do list

01 _____
02 _____
03 _____
04 _____
05 _____
06 _____
07 _____

Notes

_____
_____
_____
_____
_____
_____
_____
_____
_____
_____
_____
_____

Sunday

Monday

Tuesday

Wednesday

Thursday

Friday

Saturday

Weekly

Goals for this week

01 _____
02 _____
03 _____
04 _____
05 _____
06 _____
07 _____

To do list

01 _____
02 _____
03 _____
04 _____
05 _____
06 _____
07 _____

Notes

_____
_____
_____
_____
_____
_____
_____
_____
_____
_____
_____

Sunday

Monday

Tuesday

Wednesday

Thursday

Friday

Saturday

Weekly

Goals for this week

01 _____
02 _____
03 _____
04 _____
05 _____
06 _____
07 _____

To do list

01 _____
02 _____
03 _____
04 _____
05 _____
06 _____
07 _____

Notes

_____
_____
_____
_____
_____
_____
_____
_____
_____
_____
_____
_____

Sunday

Monday

Tuesday

Wednesday

Thursday

Friday

Saturday

Weekly

Planner

Goals for this week

01
02
03
04
05
06
07

To do list

01
02
03
04
05
06
07

Notes

Sunday

Monday

Tuesday

Wednesday

Thursday

Friday

Saturday

Weekly

Goals for this week

01 _____
02 _____
03 _____
04 _____
05 _____
06 _____
07 _____

To do list

01 _____
02 _____
03 _____
04 _____
05 _____
06 _____
07 _____

Notes

_____
_____
_____
_____
_____
_____
_____
_____
_____
_____
_____
_____

Sunday

Monday

Tuesday

Wednesday

Thursday

Friday

Saturday

June 2024

Planner

SUNDAY	MONDAY	TUESDAY	WEDNESDAY	THURSDAY	FRIDAY	SATURDAY
26	27	28	29	30	31	01
02	03	04	05	06	07	08
09	10	11	12	13	14	15
16	17	18	19	20	21	22
23	24	25	26	27	28	29
30	01	02	03	04	05	06

JUNE GOALS

GOAL

STRATEGY

_____
_____
_____
_____
_____
_____
_____
_____
_____
_____

ACTION STEPS

1 _____
2 _____
3 _____
4 _____
5 _____

Created   /   /   To Achieve By   /   /   Achieved ◯

GOAL

STRATEGY

_____
_____
_____
_____
_____
_____
_____
_____
_____
_____

ACTION STEPS

1 _____
2 _____
3 _____
4 _____
5 _____

Created   /   /   To Achieve By   /   /   Achieved ◯

Weekly

Planner

Goals for this week

01 _____
02 _____
03 _____
04 _____
05 _____
06 _____
07 _____

To do list

01 _____
02 _____
03 _____
04 _____
05 _____
06 _____
07 _____

Notes

_____
_____
_____
_____
_____
_____
_____
_____
_____
_____
_____

Sunday

Monday

Tuesday

Wednesday

Thursday

Friday

Saturday

Weekly

Goals for this week

01 _____
02 _____
03 _____
04 _____
05 _____
06 _____
07 _____

To do list

01 _____
02 _____
03 _____
04 _____
05 _____
06 _____
07 _____

Notes

_____
_____
_____
_____
_____
_____
_____
_____
_____
_____
_____

Sunday

Monday

Tuesday

Wednesday

Thursday

Friday

Saturday

Weekly
Planner

Goals for this week

01	
02	
03	
04	
05	
06	
07	

To do list

01	
02	
03	
04	
05	
06	
07	

Notes

_____
_____
_____
_____
_____
_____
_____
_____
_____
_____
_____

Sunday

Monday

Tuesday

Wednesday

Thursday

Friday

Saturday

Weekly

Goals for this week

01 _____
02 _____
03 _____
04 _____
05 _____
06 _____
07 _____

To do list

01 _____
02 _____
03 _____
04 _____
05 _____
06 _____
07 _____

Notes

_____
_____
_____
_____
_____
_____
_____
_____
_____
_____
_____
_____

Sunday

Monday

Tuesday

Wednesday

Thursday

Friday

Saturday

Weekly
Planner

Goals for this week

01 _____
02 _____
03 _____
04 _____
05 _____
06 _____
07 _____

To do list

01 _____
02 _____
03 _____
04 _____
05 _____
06 _____
07 _____

Notes

_____
_____
_____
_____
_____
_____
_____
_____
_____
_____
_____

Sunday

Monday

Tuesday

Wednesday

Thursday

Friday

Saturday

July 2024

Planner

SUNDAY	MONDAY	TUESDAY	WEDNESDAY	THURSDAY	FRIDAY	SATURDAY
30	01	02	03	04	05	06
07	08	09	10	11	12	13
14	15	16	17	18	19	20
21	22	23	24	25	26	27
28	29	30	31	01	02	03

JULY GOALS

GOAL

STRATEGY

ACTION STEPS

1
2
3
4
5

Created   /   /   To Achieve By   /   /   Achieved ◯

GOAL

STRATEGY

ACTION STEPS

1
2
3
4
5

Created   /   /   To Achieve By   /   /   Achieved ◯

Weekly

Goals for this week

01
02
03
04
05
06
07

To do list

01
02
03
04
05
06
07

Notes

Sunday

Monday

Tuesday

Wednesday

Thursday

Friday

Saturday

Weekly

Goals for this week

01	_____
02	_____
03	_____
04	_____
05	_____
06	_____
07	_____

To do list

01	_____
02	_____
03	_____
04	_____
05	_____
06	_____
07	_____

Notes

_____
_____
_____
_____
_____
_____
_____
_____
_____
_____
_____
_____

Sunday

Monday

Tuesday

Wednesday

Thursday

Friday

Saturday

Weekly

Goals for this week

01 _____
02 _____
03 _____
04 _____
05 _____
06 _____
07 _____

To do list

01 _____
02 _____
03 _____
04 _____
05 _____
06 _____
07 _____

Notes

_____
_____
_____
_____
_____
_____
_____
_____
_____
_____
_____
_____

Sunday

Monday

Tuesday

Wednesday

Thursday

Friday

Saturday

Weekly

Planner

Goals for this week

01 _____
02 _____
03 _____
04 _____
05 _____
06 _____
07 _____

To do list

01 _____
02 _____
03 _____
04 _____
05 _____
06 _____
07 _____

Notes

_____
_____
_____
_____
_____
_____
_____
_____
_____
_____
_____
_____

Sunday

Monday

Tuesday

Wednesday

Thursday

Friday

Saturday

Weekly

Goals for this week

01 _____
02 _____
03 _____
04 _____
05 _____
06 _____
07 _____

To do list

01 _____
02 _____
03 _____
04 _____
05 _____
06 _____
07 _____

Notes

_____
_____
_____
_____
_____
_____
_____
_____
_____
_____
_____

Sunday

Monday

Tuesday

Wednesday

Thursday

Friday

Saturday

August 2024

Planner

SUNDAY	MONDAY	TUESDAY	WEDNESDAY	THURSDAY	FRIDAY	SATURDAY
28	29	30	31	01	02	03
04	05	06	07	08	09	10
11	12	13	14	15	16	17
18	19	20	21	22	23	24
25	26	27	28	29	30	31

AUGUST GOALS

GOAL

STRATEGY

ACTION STEPS

1
2
3
4
5

Created   /   /   To Achieve By   /   /   Achieved ◯

GOAL

STRATEGY

ACTION STEPS

1
2
3
4
5

Created   /   /   To Achieve By   /   /   Achieved ◯

Weekly

Goals for this week

01 _____
02 _____
03 _____
04 _____
05 _____
06 _____
07 _____

To do list

01 _____
02 _____
03 _____
04 _____
05 _____
06 _____
07 _____

Notes

_____
_____
_____
_____
_____
_____
_____
_____
_____
_____
_____

Sunday

Monday

Tuesday

Wednesday

Thursday

Friday

Saturday

Weekly

Goals for this week

01 _____
02 _____
03 _____
04 _____
05 _____
06 _____
07 _____

To do list

01 _____
02 _____
03 _____
04 _____
05 _____
06 _____
07 _____

Notes

_____
_____
_____
_____
_____
_____
_____
_____
_____
_____
_____
_____

Sunday

Monday

Tuesday

Wednesday

Thursday

Friday

Saturday

Weekly

Planner

Goals for this week

01 _____
02 _____
03 _____
04 _____
05 _____
06 _____
07 _____

To do list

01 _____
02 _____
03 _____
04 _____
05 _____
06 _____
07 _____

Notes

_____
_____
_____
_____
_____
_____
_____
_____
_____
_____
_____
_____

Sunday

Monday

Tuesday

Wednesday

Thursday

Friday

Saturday

Weekly

Goals for this week

01 _____
02 _____
03 _____
04 _____
05 _____
06 _____
07 _____

To do list

01 _____
02 _____
03 _____
04 _____
05 _____
06 _____
07 _____

Notes

_____
_____
_____
_____
_____
_____
_____
_____
_____
_____
_____
_____

Sunday

Monday

Tuesday

Wednesday

Thursday

Friday

Saturday

Weekly

Goals for this week

01 _____
02 _____
03 _____
04 _____
05 _____
06 _____
07 _____

To do list

01 _____
02 _____
03 _____
04 _____
05 _____
06 _____
07 _____

Notes

_____
_____
_____
_____
_____
_____
_____
_____
_____
_____
_____
_____

Sunday

Monday

Tuesday

Wednesday

Thursday

Friday

Saturday

September 2024

Planner

SUNDAY	MONDAY	TUESDAY	WEDNESDAY	THURSDAY	FRIDAY	SATURDAY
01	02	03	04	05	06	07
08	09	10	11	12	13	14
15	16	17	18	19	20	21
22	23	24	25	26	27	28
29	30	01	02	03	04	05

SEPTEMBER GOALS

GOAL

STRATEGY

_____
_____
_____
_____
_____
_____
_____

ACTION STEPS

1 _____
2 _____
3 _____
4 _____
5 _____

_____
_____
_____
_____
_____

Created   /   /   To Achieve By   /   /   Achieved ○

GOAL

STRATEGY

_____
_____
_____
_____
_____
_____
_____

ACTION STEPS

1 _____
2 _____
3 _____
4 _____
5 _____

_____
_____
_____
_____
_____

Created   /   /   To Achieve By   /   /   Achieved ○

Weekly

Goals for this week

01 _____
02 _____
03 _____
04 _____
05 _____
06 _____
07 _____

To do list

01 _____
02 _____
03 _____
04 _____
05 _____
06 _____
07 _____

Notes

_____
_____
_____
_____
_____
_____
_____
_____
_____
_____
_____
_____

Sunday

Monday

Tuesday

Wednesday

Thursday

Friday

Saturday

Weekly

Goals for this week

01 _____
02 _____
03 _____
04 _____
05 _____
06 _____
07 _____

To do list

01 _____
02 _____
03 _____
04 _____
05 _____
06 _____
07 _____

Notes

_____
_____
_____
_____
_____
_____
_____
_____
_____
_____
_____

Sunday

Monday

Tuesday

Wednesday

Thursday

Friday

Saturday

Weekly

Goals for this week

01 _____
02 _____
03 _____
04 _____
05 _____
06 _____
07 _____

To do list

01 _____
02 _____
03 _____
04 _____
05 _____
06 _____
07 _____

Notes

_____
_____
_____
_____
_____
_____
_____
_____
_____
_____
_____
_____

Sunday

Monday

Tuesday

Wednesday

Thursday

Friday

Saturday

Weekly

Goals for this week

01 _____
02 _____
03 _____
04 _____
05 _____
06 _____
07 _____

To do list

01 _____
02 _____
03 _____
04 _____
05 _____
06 _____
07 _____

Notes

_____
_____
_____
_____
_____
_____
_____
_____
_____
_____
_____

Sunday

Monday

Tuesday

Wednesday

Thursday

Friday

Saturday

Weekly

Goals for this week

01 _____
02 _____
03 _____
04 _____
05 _____
06 _____
07 _____

To do list

01 _____
02 _____
03 _____
04 _____
05 _____
06 _____
07 _____

Notes

_____
_____
_____
_____
_____
_____
_____
_____
_____
_____
_____
_____

Sunday

Monday

Tuesday

Wednesday

Thursday

Friday

Saturday

October 2024

Planner

SUNDAY	MONDAY	TUESDAY	WEDNESDAY	THURSDAY	FRIDAY	SATURDAY
29	30	01	02	03	04	05
06	07	08	09	10	11	12
13	14	15	16	17	18	19
20	21	22	23	24	25	26
27	28	29	30	31	01	02

OCTOBER GOALS

GOAL

STRATEGY

ACTION STEPS

1
2
3
4
5

Created   /   /   To Achieve By   /   /   Achieved ◯

GOAL

STRATEGY

ACTION STEPS

1
2
3
4
5

Created   /   /   To Achieve By   /   /   Achieved ◯

Weekly

Goals for this week

01 _____
02 _____
03 _____
04 _____
05 _____
06 _____
07 _____

To do list

01 _____
02 _____
03 _____
04 _____
05 _____
06 _____
07 _____

Notes

_____
_____
_____
_____
_____
_____
_____
_____
_____
_____
_____
_____

Sunday

Monday

Tuesday

Wednesday

Thursday

Friday

Saturday

Weekly
Planner

Goals for this week

01
02
03
04
05
06
07

To do list

01
02
03
04
05
06
07

Notes

Sunday

Monday

Tuesday

Wednesday

Thursday

Friday

Saturday

Weekly

Goals for this week

01 _____
02 _____
03 _____
04 _____
05 _____
06 _____
07 _____

To do list

01 _____
02 _____
03 _____
04 _____
05 _____
06 _____
07 _____

Notes

_____
_____
_____
_____
_____
_____
_____
_____
_____
_____
_____
_____

Sunday

Monday

Tuesday

Wednesday

Thursday

Friday

Saturday

Weekly

Goals for this week

01 _____
02 _____
03 _____
04 _____
05 _____
06 _____
07 _____

To do list

01 _____
02 _____
03 _____
04 _____
05 _____
06 _____
07 _____

Notes

_____
_____
_____
_____
_____
_____
_____
_____
_____
_____
_____
_____

Sunday

Monday

Tuesday

Wednesday

Thursday

Friday

Saturday

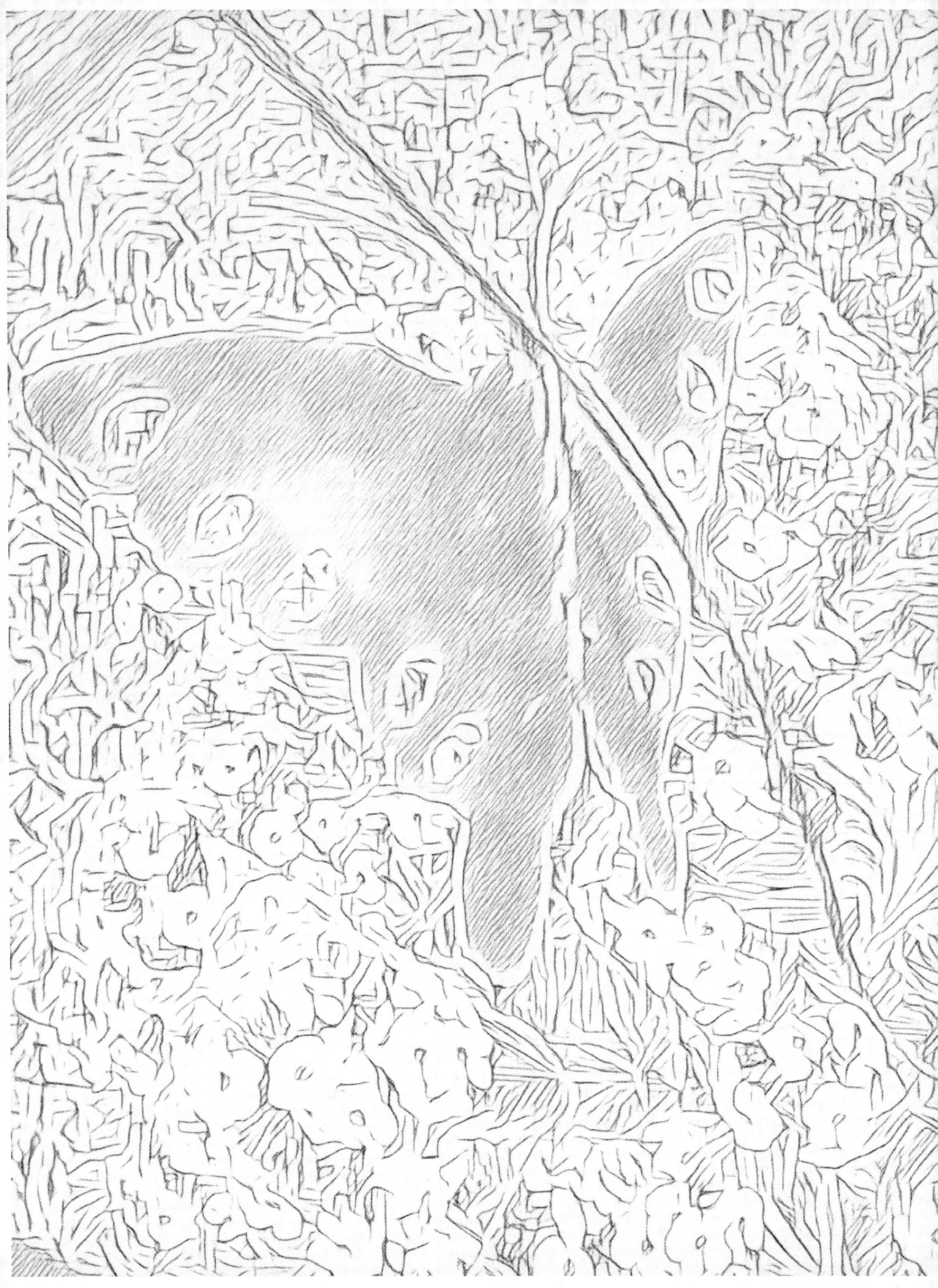

Weekly

Goals for this week

01	
02	
03	
04	
05	
06	
07	

To do list

01	
02	
03	
04	
05	
06	
07	

Notes

_____

_____

_____

_____

_____

_____

_____

_____

_____

_____

Sunday

Monday

Tuesday

Wednesday

Thursday

Friday

Saturday

November 2024

Planner

SUNDAY	MONDAY	TUESDAY	WEDNESDAY	THURSDAY	FRIDAY	SATURDAY
27	28	29	30	31	01	02
03	04	05	06	07	08	09
10	11	12	13	14	15	16
17	18	19	20	21	22	23
24	25	26	27	28	29	30

NOVEMBER GOALS

GOAL

STRATEGY

ACTION STEPS

1
2
3
4
5

Created   /   /   To Achieve By   /   /   Achieved ◯

GOAL

STRATEGY

ACTION STEPS

1
2
3
4
5

Created   /   /   To Achieve By   /   /   Achieved ◯

Weekly

Goals for this week

01 _____
02 _____
03 _____
04 _____
05 _____
06 _____
07 _____

To do list

01 _____
02 _____
03 _____
04 _____
05 _____
06 _____
07 _____

Notes

_____
_____
_____
_____
_____
_____
_____
_____
_____
_____
_____

Sunday

Monday

Tuesday

Wednesday

Thursday

Friday

Saturday

Weekly

Goals for this week

01 _____
02 _____
03 _____
04 _____
05 _____
06 _____
07 _____

To do list

01 _____
02 _____
03 _____
04 _____
05 _____
06 _____
07 _____

Notes

_____
_____
_____
_____
_____
_____
_____
_____
_____
_____
_____
_____

Sunday

Monday

Tuesday

Wednesday

Thursday

Friday

Saturday

Weekly

Goals for this week

01 _____
02 _____
03 _____
04 _____
05 _____
06 _____
07 _____

To do list

01 _____
02 _____
03 _____
04 _____
05 _____
06 _____
07 _____

Notes

_____
_____
_____
_____
_____
_____
_____
_____
_____
_____
_____
_____

Sunday

Monday

Tuesday

Wednesday

Thursday

Friday

Saturday

Weekly

Goals for this week

01	
02	
03	
04	
05	
06	
07	

To do list

01	
02	
03	
04	
05	
06	
07	

Notes

Sunday

Monday

Tuesday

Wednesday

Thursday

Friday

Saturday

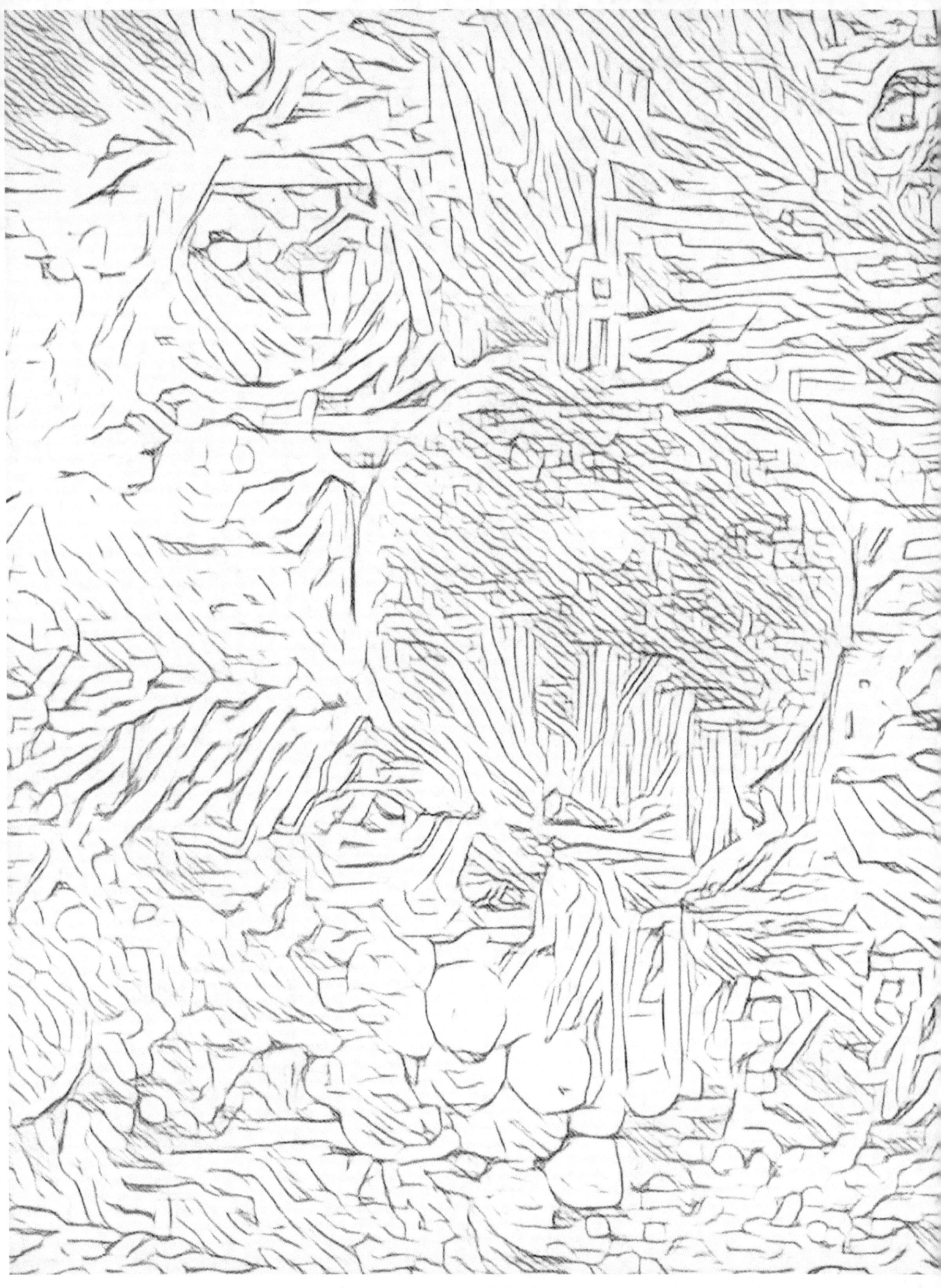

Weekly

Goals for this week

01 _____
02 _____
03 _____
04 _____
05 _____
06 _____
07 _____

To do list

01 _____
02 _____
03 _____
04 _____
05 _____
06 _____
07 _____

Notes

_____
_____
_____
_____
_____
_____
_____
_____
_____
_____
_____
_____

Sunday

Monday

Tuesday

Wednesday

Thursday

Friday

Saturday

December 2024

Planner

SUNDAY	MONDAY	TUESDAY	WEDNESDAY	THURSDAY	FRIDAY	SATURDAY
01	02	03	04	05	06	07
08	09	10	11	12	13	14
15	16	17	18	19	20	21
22	23	24	25	26	27	28
29	30	31	01	02	03	04

DECEMBER GOALS

GOAL

STRATEGY

ACTION STEPS

1
2
3
4
5

Created   /   /   To Achieve By   /   /   Achieved ◯

GOAL

STRATEGY

ACTION STEPS

1
2
3
4
5

Created   /   /   To Achieve By   /   /   Achieved ◯

Weekly

Goals for this week

01 _____
02 _____
03 _____
04 _____
05 _____
06 _____
07 _____

To do list

01 _____
02 _____
03 _____
04 _____
05 _____
06 _____
07 _____

Notes

_____
_____
_____
_____
_____
_____
_____
_____
_____
_____

Sunday

Monday

Tuesday

Wednesday

Thursday

Friday

Saturday

Weekly

Goals for this week

01 _____
02 _____
03 _____
04 _____
05 _____
06 _____
07 _____

To do list

01 _____
02 _____
03 _____
04 _____
05 _____
06 _____
07 _____

Notes

_____
_____
_____
_____
_____
_____
_____
_____
_____
_____
_____

Sunday

Monday

Tuesday

Wednesday

Thursday

Friday

Saturday

Weekly

Goals for this week

01	
02	
03	
04	
05	
06	
07	

To do list

01	
02	
03	
04	
05	
06	
07	

Notes

Sunday

Monday

Tuesday

Wednesday

Thursday

Friday

Saturday

Weekly

Goals for this week

01 _____
02 _____
03 _____
04 _____
05 _____
06 _____
07 _____

To do list

01 _____
02 _____
03 _____
04 _____
05 _____
06 _____
07 _____

Notes

_____
_____
_____
_____
_____
_____
_____
_____
_____
_____
_____

Sunday

Monday

Tuesday

Wednesday

Thursday

Friday

Saturday

Weekly
Planner

Goals for this week

01 _____
02 _____
03 _____
04 _____
05 _____
06 _____
07 _____

To do list

01 _____
02 _____
03 _____
04 _____
05 _____
06 _____
07 _____

Notes

_____
_____
_____
_____
_____
_____
_____
_____
_____
_____
_____
_____

Sunday

Monday

Tuesday

Wednesday

Thursday

Friday

Saturday

2024 REFLECTIONS

HIGHLIGHTS OF THE YEAR
- Note down the most memorable and significant events of the year.

CHALLENGES OVERCOME
- Reflect on the challenges faced and how they were overcome.

THINGS I'M GRATEFUL FOR
- Write a list to acknowledge what you're thankful for in the year.

GOALS FOR NEXT YEAR
- Set a few important goals for the upcoming year.

PERSONAL DEVELOPMENT
- Reflect on personal growth and areas for improvement.

RELATIONSHIPS
- Set goals related to family, friends, or social life.

AT A GLANCE

JAN

S	M	T	W	T	F	S
			1	2	3	4
5	6	7	8	9	10	11
12	13	14	15	16	17	18
19	20	21	22	23	24	25
26	27	28	29	30	31	

FEB

S	M	T	W	T	F	S
						1
2	3	4	5	6	7	8
9	10	11	12	13	14	15
16	17	18	19	20	21	22
23	24	25	26	27	28	

MAR

S	M	T	W	T	F	S
						1
2	3	4	5	6	7	8
9	10	11	12	13	14	15
16	17	18	19	20	21	22
23	24	25	26	27	28	29
30	31					

APR

S	M	T	W	T	F	S
		1	2	3	4	5
6	7	8	9	10	11	12
13	14	15	16	17	18	19
20	21	22	23	24	25	26
27	28	29	30			

MAY

S	M	T	W	T	F	S
				1	2	3
4	5	6	7	8	9	10
11	12	13	14	15	16	17
18	19	20	21	22	23	24
25	26	27	28	29	30	31

JUN

S	M	T	W	T	F	S
1	2	3	4	5	6	7
8	9	10	11	12	13	14
15	16	17	18	19	20	21
22	23	24	25	26	27	28
29	30					

JUL

S	M	T	W	T	F	S
		1	2	3	4	5
6	7	8	9	10	11	12
13	14	15	16	17	18	19
20	21	22	23	24	25	26
27	28	29	30	31		

AUG

S	M	T	W	T	F	S
					1	2
3	4	5	6	7	8	9
10	11	12	13	14	15	16
17	18	19	20	21	22	23
24	25	26	27	28	29	30
31						

SEP

S	M	T	W	T	F	S
	1	2	3	4	5	6
7	8	9	10	11	12	13
14	15	16	17	18	19	20
21	22	23	24	25	26	27
28	29	30				

OCT

S	M	T	W	T	F	S
			1	2	3	4
5	6	7	8	9	10	11
12	13	14	15	16	17	18
19	20	21	22	23	24	25
26	27	28	29	30	31	

NOV

S	M	T	W	T	F	S
						1
2	3	4	5	6	7	8
9	10	11	12	13	14	15
16	17	18	19	20	21	22
23	24	25	26	27	28	29
30						

DEC

S	M	T	W	T	F	S
	1	2	3	4	5	6
7	8	9	10	11	12	13
14	15	16	17	18	19	20
21	22	23	24	25	26	27
28	29	30	31			

Thank You!

I hope you enjoyed this 2024 coloring goal planner!

Look out for the 2025 version

If you loved it, don't forget to leave a review!

AMANDA
AUTHOR

Other Resources

For a complete list of products, visit my Amazon Author Page

You can find more photographer tools, digital products, print products and more in my Etsy Shop